# Brothers

# Brothers

*Lost of Childhood*

E. B. Johnston

authorHOUSE®

AuthorHouse™
1663 Liberty Drive
Bloomington, IN 47403
www.authorhouse.com
Phone: 1-800-839-8640

Published by AuthorHouse    03/30/2012

ISBN: 978-1-4685-6456-3 (sc)
ISBN: 978-1-4685-6455-6 (hc)
ISBN: 978-1-4685-6454-9 (e)

Library of Congress Control Number: 2012904860

Sitting here on top of the world, remembering my life as I know it, the cold wind blowing across the valley and it's January first and I deciding it was time for me to release my anger, fears, sorrow and pain.

My life wasn't so simple nor was it what most would say happy. I can remember back to when I was six years old, a skinny, blonde haired and green eyed and just full of life.

My brother's;

Jason a selfish and spoiled person, only thinking of himself and always getting what he wants. My brother Gary; a lone wolf, a loner sort of speak, trouble in some people's eyes. Then there was David; little four year old who was always active, happy, and always following me around.

One day my mom and dad were arguing over money and beer, and who drank way to many beers or how much was spent! I heard my dad say "Debra, there are plenty of beers left, what's the problem?" "No there aren't!" In a loud, angry voice my mom replied "You got the last one?" My dad said "Please, not in front of the boys, ok?" "To hell with the boys" she said; as she went walking out the door, slamming it with such force, it knocked a picture off the wall.

I walked over to David and said "Let's go into the bedroom and play" He took my hand and I guided him away. As my dad stood in the living room bracing for what's to come. Just as I shut the bedroom door my mom entered the house and I heard my dad say "Debra, please don't do that" and all hell broke loose. I took David and snuggled in the corner with him and said "Stay here and you will be ok".

I walked over to the door and reached to lock it and it opened, my dad came in first "Not in front of the boys!" Mom continued to throw blows and all of a sudden I yelled out "STOP IT! STOP IT! RIGHT NOW OR I'M GOING TO CALL THE COPS!"

My mom turned and looked at me, "Go ahead, you little son of a bitch call the cops and see what happens". At this moment fear entered my body. I just knew I was going to get it for sure. My dad pushes his way past my mom; "I will deal with you later".

She looked at me as I coward deeper in the corner, my dad said, "Let's go outside and discuss this Debra" as he walked out the front door my mom continued to follow. You could her voice all the way to the back of the house, screaming, cursing and suddenly there was a silence.

I thought thank god it's over! Boy was I wrong. CRASH I heard shattering glass; my mom took a baseball bat and broke the windshield in the car. Dad yelled out, "You crazy bitch, what's wrong with you?"

Then turned the bat on him, he ran around the car as he says "Put the bat down! Put it down Debra". He said time and time again.

Mom stopped, my dad out of breath asked "Are you done now?" she didn't say a word, as I watched out of the bedroom window she walked over to the porch and sat down.

*Something out of the corner of my eye caught my attention; it was smoke, my dad asked "Where are Gary and Jason?" Mom said with an exhausted look on her face "Jason is with his cousins and Gary is around here somewhere" my dad looked up "OMG we got to find Gary?" I ran out of the house I said "I saw Gary walking into field and that is where the smoke is coming from".*

*As we ran to field, there it was; flames everywhere. "Gary" I screamed out "Gary" my dad yelled with fear in his voice "Answer me boy?" And around the corner he walking like nothing ever happened.*

*I knew right then he was the reason and wow, was he going to get it; in a bad way! He walked slowly over to dad "I'm sorry" He said repeatedly over and over, "I'm sorry". My dad said "Boys, start getting the hose out". Our neighbors came running out with water hoses in hand, everyone was hurrying and skimping to get the flames out.*

*Everyone's houses was in danger, they fought the flames until the fire department showed up and put it out. The fireman in charge walked over and asked "Does anyone know how this started? Did anyone see anything at all?"*

No one spoke up or came forward. My dad stood in silence knowing what just happened, but it was his own son, and he will deal with it his way.

And did he ever, you could hear the belt connect to Gary, it was terrifying and it put chills on my skin, as I heard the screams come from the back room. That went on for almost an hour but it seemed like an eternity to me.

Gary laying in his bed, bleeding and in pain, looking at me with tears in his eyes "Help me Bob, please" My dad walked in "Bob, if you don't want the same thing, you will leave this room and not come back in here till I say you can". I walked out looking over my shoulder with sorrow and tears in my eyes for Gary, no matter what he done he was still my brother and I loved him.

When I got back to my room David sitting on floor playing, I sat down beside him, "So David, what would you like to play?" He smiled and threw a ball at me. Off in the distance I could hear mom and dad's voices "What do you want to do about Gary?" My mom said with anger in her voice. "I already handled it Debra, let it go" "Let it go, did you say let it go?" Mom replied and I could hear the sarcasm building and here we go again, I thought to myself.

"David come here let's turn on the radio and listen to some music" I turned the radio up just enough so he wouldn't have to hear the arguing again. I took him by the hands and started dancing with him; he smiled and started rocking back and forth laughing and jumping. The arguing got louder, I could hear glass breaking and my dad saying "Ok bitch, if that's how you want it! Fine let's do this" So off they went destroying everything in the house; throwing things at one another, bloody and drunk it continued for almost two hours, until one of the neighbors called the cops.

Scared to death, David and I were sitting in the closet, crying hoping someone would come help us. Gary already crawled out of his bedroom window and went to his friend's house. It got silent, I could hear footsteps walk into my room, the door knob to the closet turning I looked up and it was a policeman and our neighbor "Come here babies, are you ok? Now no one will hurt you"

As we walked out of the closet, Mr. Hunt; our neighbor reached down and picked me up and his wife took David in her arms, we walked out of the house. Both mom and dad were in the back of two police cruisers, still arguing with each other through the glass. Come on boys, you don't need to see that.

As we walked past the cars I looked over Mr. Hunt's shoulder at my parents in the cruisers, thinking I would never see them again. I reached out for my dad; he stopped yelling and dropped his head like he didn't want me to see him.

As we walked into the front door of the Hunt's, Mrs. Hunt said "What about the other two boys?" Mr. Hunt sat me down in a chair "I will be right back little man, stay right here" He turned and walked out. "Are you boy's hungry?" Mrs. Hunt asked, I said "Yes ma'am" She smiled and made us some ravioli.

Just as we sat down to eat, Mr. Hunt walked in "The other two boys are safe" and quickly I asked "Am I going to see my brothers again?" With tears in my eyes and my lips quivering he said; "Of course".

Mr. Hunt quickly distracted me by asking "Hey, would you boys like to come live with Mrs. Hunt and myself?" I immediately asked "Can David come too?" He smiled "Yes, of course he can" I looked at David and he was crying as Mrs. Hunt was trying to feed him. "David I'm right here, it will be ok" I lifted my chocolate milk to my lips "Try this David its great" He lifted the cup to his mouth and it started dribbling down his chin, "Here let me give you this straw" he took the straw and smiled. Mrs. Hunt smiled at us "Its bedtime boys, so let's tuck you in for the night."

Mr. Hunt went into the back room and brought out blankets, while David and I finished eating. Wow, did David make a mess. Mrs. Hunt laughed, "Young man you must of been very hungry" as she cleaned him up. Mr. Hunt made us a bed on the floor and said "Come here boys? Let's get you two snuggled in for the night".

"Good night boys" Mrs. Hunt said as she walked by and smiled at us. Mr. Hunt said "Has anyone ever read you a book"? As he reached for one and started reading to me and David, we're tired and bellies full, it didn't take long for us to fall fast asleep.

It was about two in the morning when I woke up to their voices talking in the other room, I heard her say "Why can't we just keep them? Let's go to the courthouse tomorrow and see what we can do"? And her husband replied "Honey, I wish we could, I really do, but we just don't have the room or money to take them both". I rose up and started to walk into their room, but changed my mind as I approached their door, so I turned around and went back and laid down beside David, put my arm over him and whispered "We stay together, no matter what, no matter what", as I closed my eyes and fell back asleep.

The next morning I could smell something I haven't smelled in a long time, breakfast! "David, wake up, wake up! Do you smell that"? Wow, it was amazing, we both jumped up and ran to the kitchen, sat down and started to help ourselves. "Young men; not till we give thanks to the lord boys", I looked confused; "The lord! Who is that"? I asked

Mr. Hunt looked at me and smiled "Who is the lord? He is the reason we have this food, the lord is the reason we have air, night and day. The lord created this world we live in, the lord created us". I thought to myself if the lord created me, then why is the lord torturing me? Was I bad kid? Did I do something wrong?

I asked "Will the lord help my mom and dad not fights anymore"? He looked at me and said "Bobby, boy the lord works in mysterious ways, I sure hope so".

At this time I said "I hate the fighting". Mrs. Hunt with tears in her eyes said "Let's give thanks now".

When we finished breakfast, we heard a knock, when Mrs. Hunt opened the door it was a policeman and a man in a suit. One of them said "Hi there boys, how are you this morning"? I knew it wasn't a good morning, I found out the man in the suit was a case worker from the Child and Family Services.

They were there to take us away? I started crying "Please! Please, don't take my brother away from me? Please, don't separate us? He is all I got".

Mrs. Hunt started crying and said "Is there any way we could keep them until their parents get their lives right"? The case worker stood there for a moment and smiled and said "Sure, but I will check in on them to make sure they are taken care off". I ran over to Mrs. Hunt and all I can say was "Thank you, thank you and thank you!"

She pulled me in close with David in her arms and said "See, god works in mysterious ways" and turned and we walked inside.

We had so much fun with the Hunts, we played games, went to church, done things I only heard of other kids doing, I loved it.

*We were outside in the back yard "BOB, DAVID, and WHERE ARE YOU BOYS AT"? A very familiar voice from the distant; it sounded, it was like my stomach dropped. I turned and looked it was my mom and dad.*

*I didn't want to leave; I clanged to Mrs. Hunt's leg looking up at her, all I could say was "I don't want to go! Please, don't make me! Please" Poor Mrs. Hunt said "You have to Bob, they are your parents". I hung on for dear life.*

*At this time I heard my mom's voice saying "Come on son, it's ok, mama is here now!" I cried as they put us in the car. When we got home my mom opened the door and said get out, I reached up and grabbed the opening and my mom slammed the door shut on my hand. The pain was so sharp I screamed; "Open the door, open the door" She continued to walk into the house. My brother Gary came running out of the house opened the door "Are you ok?" he asked.*

*My fingers, bleeding, and throbbing in pain. I wrapped my hand in my shirt and ran in the house. Ran cold water over it, then I heard "Shut up boy, it didn't hurt that bad! Go to your room and think about how bad you made me and your dad look? Acting that* way in front of those people". Crying in pain I knew if I didn't do as she ask I would pay the price, so I went to my room and shut the door.

I said to Gary "Nothing has changed, has it?", "No, it's going to get worse before it gets better, so just suck it up and be a man". I stayed in my room all day.

David sat with our dad for awhile, before coming in the room to lay down. As I asked "Are you ok David", he just turned over and felt asleep. Soon after I joined him I dreamed of being with the Hunts again, they were nice people and I missed them.

The next day my dad woke us all up "Boys pack some things up, we are going camping", excited and surprised I helped David pack some things and then I packed. We have never been camping, just heard my dad talk about how much fun it was. So mom and the kids loaded up and off we went, excited and eager we pulled up to the lake. Wow it was big and beautiful and off in the distance we could see another car coming down the path. My dad behind them on his motor cycle it was my grandparents.

My grand dad gets out of the car "Hey there boys, how have ya'all been doing?" I yelled out "paw paw, mawmaw" with a huge smile on my face I ran to them.

My pawpaw picked me up "How you doing boy" and squeezed me so tight and I couldn't breathe but I didn't care, he was my hero and stayed my hero my whole life. "Bumper, come with me" he smiled and reached down for my hand, "Help this old man with his stuff" so we unloaded their car.

I looked in the trunk as he opened it and there were jugs of what I thought was water, he said "Whoa boy you're not old enough for that yet" smiling and I said "Old enough for what pawpaw? It's just water!" Looking up at him with a confused look. "Oh no son, that's fire water, glimming sun light in a jug ok?" Now I was really confused and he laughed "Come on lets you and I go fishing" as he handed me a rod and reel.

Later that day all the adults were sitting around the camp fire drinking what pawpaw called fire water. As the evening got closer to darkness the fire was blazing I sat between my pawpaw and my dad. I felt like a prince, sitting between to kings. My dad looked at my pawpaw and said "You know Billy even though you were a boxing champ in the Navy, I can still take you" he went on and on and on till my pawpaw looked at me and said "Bumper, why don't you go get a couple towels for this old timer?" I got up and started walking to the tent the next thing I knew my dad was knocked cold and my pawpaw was sitting back down to take another drink.

My mom ran over "Richard, are you ok? Wake up? I went behind the car and laughed so hard I peeweed my pants, how I loved my pawpaw. I took the towel back to the fire, handed to pawpaw and he helped my dad up, "Richard, are you ok? I'm sorry but you just don't talk about the Navy", my pawpaw walked away and I followed him to the edge of the lake bank.

"Pawpaw, why did you knock my dad out?" and he said "Sit down here beside me son, and I will tell you; see I was in Pearl Harbor when it was attacked, a lot of good men died that day and everyone of those heroes should be remembered just as that; heroes."

He didn't say much after that, after about thirty minutes later he stood up and said here hold this and handed me his empty cup,

SPLASH he leaped off the bank into the water I yelled "HELP, HELP, pawpaw is drowning!" My dad came running with my mom right behind him. "Where is Billy?" My dad asked, I said "Down there, in the water."

He leaped off the bank landed feet first in the water. Lifted my pawpaw up and next thing I knew my pawpaw grabbed my dad "Come on Richard let's do the back stroke together", shocked and surprised I stood there for a second before everyone started laughing and thought what was so funny? I was scared to death I thought I lost my pawpaw.

The next morning after all the excitement my dad decided he wanted to ride his Harley around the lake; apparently he had a little too much to drink because he was still pretty toasted. We could hear him off in the distance riding on the old dirt road we came in on.

The engine of the bike roaring through the woods, he finally topped the hill and road up to where we were standing "Boys, make me path, I'm going to jump this lake". He turned and spun off up the hill, my mom standing down by the water with my grandparents talking.

We started clearing him a path as he disappeared over the hill top, as we got the last stick out of the way, we could hear him racing towards the water, he topped the hill just hauling butt, as fast as he could.

My mom and grandparents yelled out "STOP, RICHARD STOP!" He yelled out "Yeee haaww" Just as he went air born he dropped as fast, he went up the bike hit the water first then my dad. My mom screamed out "Oh my god, what the hell were you thinking?" My dad laughing as he swam back to the shore. That was great, as he stood there dripping wet, he looked out towards the lake and said "What the hell did I just do?" And started running back into the water.

My brothers and I took off laughing so hard "Wow that was so cool!" Gary said David holding my hand looked up at me with a stick in his hand smiling, Jason laughing, I sat down, along with David looking at the stick he had. "What's that you got there?" I asked and he waved it around laughing.

"Let's load up boys, camping is over, come on now time to go home." So we packed everything up and off we went, my dad passed out in the passenger's seat not really realizing what he just done. He was not the same for a long time after that. He was silent and bitter, like he just lost his best friend. Well, in a way he did! That bike was his baby; he built it with his own two hands. I felt sad for my dad, in a way that was is baby.

It was close to time to go to school, in two days I would be starting my first day of school. My mom and dad put me a school that was in a church. I rode to school every day in taxi, it was awesome because it was my uncle that took me and picked me up. Two months into the school year I just made a 100 on a drawing I did, I was so eager to show everyone my work, my uncle looked at it and said "That's a great job little man, your parents are going to be proud". Smiling I said "Yes they will Uncle Robert", he turned into my driveway and let me out "Bye Uncle Robert, have a good day at work." He said "You have a good day to little man".

I turned and took four or five steps up the drive and felt something hit me in the head and I dropped to the ground, I could hear Gary screaming for mom and dad "HELP, HELP I killed Bob, I'm so sorry Bob, I'm so sorry!" I couldn't feel anything, all I know is, I couldn't move and I was feeling very sick and blacked out, one minute I was there and the next I was somewhere else.

I remember wakening up in my mom arms, blood all over her blouse and hearing her say, "Hurry Richard, his losing a lot of blood, I don't think he is going to make it to the hospital, Hurry". I looked up at my mom and said "Mom, I will be ok," feeling like I wanted to go to sleep, she kept shaking me "Wake up, don't you fall asleep, stay awake?" My arms and legs so weak I couldn't move them, my head throbbing, I went black as we approached the hospital.

When I came to, I was laying on a hospital bed with a doctor standing over me. "Well, hello there young man, how are we feeling?" I looked around for my mom she wasn't there, my dad was sitting there with his hand on my arm "You're alright son, you will be just fine." Dazed I looked around; "Where is mom?" He said "She had to step outside."

The doctor begins looking into my eyes and checking my reflexes. My dad asked "Is he alright doc? The doctor suggested for my parents to take me home and keep a close eye on me. He also recommended that every two to three hours to see if I wake up.

"Come on son" My dad reaches out and takes me from the table, walking out of the hospital hand and hand we stop and look for my mom.

"Come on son, let's sit over here and wait for her my mom, she took the car and went to the store." When she finally did show up, she had a beer between her legs, what is that Debra and she said "I had to have something, my nerves are shot" My dad was surprised that she had the beer, "We waited here for you so you could go get beer?"

"Please dad, not tonight!" I said, he looked at me and smiled "its ok son, nothing is going to happen I promise". We loaded up in the car; my dad sat in the back seat with me and put his arm around me. As we pulled in the drive way Gary was sitting on porch waiting for us. Anxiously, he ran to my door asking "Are you ok Bob? Are you ok?" As my dad said "Gary, take your brother inside. Me and mom have to talk about something". As he took me by the hand and said "Come on Bob, I'm really sorry, I didn't mean to hurt you, and I asked "What did you hit me with?" He said he picked up a brick and he threw at me, dropping his head and handed me the brick "Go ahead, hit me go ahead hit me with this brick I deserve it".

I looked at him and smiled "I don't want to hit you Gary, I just want to go to bed, and I'm tired". He guided me down the hall and opened the door, "Go ahead, I will stay up all night with you, I will make sure you are ok"

As I laid down I could hear my dad outside my bedroom window telling my mom "If you don't get your act together I will take the boys and leave". My mom yelled at my dad and said "Go ahead take the little bastards but Jason stays here with me?" Dad replied "No Debra, I take one I take all!" As he walked away.

Mom followed him cursing him, telling him "You take those boys and I will have you arrested for kidnapping them". My dad ignoring her walking into the house and straight to the bedroom, my mom following him still, cursing and dad finally said "Shut up Debra the boys are asleep". As they continued through the night Gary never left my side, checking on me every time I moved he would ask "Are you ok" "Yes", I would reply. At about the twenty time of him asking the same thing it was starting to annoy me and I finally told him "Gary, just let me sleep ok, I'm tired and I want to sleep, ok? And he agreed with me, finally we both fell asleep.

That night mom decided to call the police on my dad, however dad decided to hide in the attic, the entrance to the attic was in my room. When the police arrived at the house, my mom who was drunk told the cops that my dad was somewhere in the house.

As they were searching they heard a loud noise. The noise was that my dad came thru the ceiling from the attic and landed on my bedroom floor. As he laid on the floor the cops said "Hey Richard, how are you". Everyone at the time thought that was quite funny and the police left with just given my parents a warning.

The next morning it was silent, no arguing, no fighting. My dad left in the middle of the night, he left us there. With the after math my mom passed out on the sofa, rolled over and started moaning "Who is fixing breakfast this morning?" As she opened her eyes Jason walked out, "What's for breakfast", Gary said "I will cook!" But there wasn't anything in kitchen to cook so I felt pretty safe from food poisoning.

My mom staggered out of the living room "Move, I will cook" So she made grits. I hated grits, after breakfast my mom told us it's time to clean house before we knew it, our dads clothes were out in the yard. "What are you doing?" I asked her. She looked at me and said "Your dad isn't coming back" Wow was she wrong, about that time my dad pulled in with the cops and said "Come on boys lets go", we went inside and got our clothes and loaded in my aunts car and off to mawmaw Jenkins we went.

It didn't take my mom long before she rounded up her brothers and came to my mawmaw's house. My dad and all of his brother's in law and my mawmaw Jenkins went into the porch and all hell broke loose. My mawmaw looked at my mom with a knife in her hands and said come on up here and I will put you out of your misery.

About the time the police showed up and took my dad off to the side now "Richard, you have to give the boys back to their mother" Dad said "Over my dead body, if I will she will hurt them" The police advise was "Richard, until she does there is nothing we can do about it, so give the boys back or go to jail" dad worried out of his mind asked "Well, what can I do to keep them safe?" The officer asked "Is the house is in your name? If so, Richard you don't have to leave, just go home it's your house". At this time my dad went into my mawmaw's house and got his clothes and followed behind us with the cops on his bumper, so my uncles won't follow him.

As we turned into the driveway, my mom stopped jumped out of the car and ran into the house and came back out as my dad pulled in, come on boys get in the house, and she rushed us like something was wrong.

Go to your rooms and don't come out till I tell you to. My dad walked into the front door and it was world war three when the cops left. The first thing we heard was the dishes flying up against the wall and we all climbed out of window and ran to the front of the house, just standing there, listening and watching the neighbors all came out and stood in the road with concern and amazement on their faces.

This is mine and this is yours, that's all we heard till finally the TV came flying out of the picture window into the yard, WHOA you could hear the neighbors sound off as it hit the ground soon after the stereo follow and with every item that flew out of window, you could hear "Oh, yeah, well this is yours" and another item came flying out of the house.

Finally, the police pulled up and stood there in the yard, the neighbors asked "Are you guys going to end this?" they replied "Nothing we can do, it's their own property they are destroying".

After about an hour of this, it got quite my dad walked out sat down on the steps and light it up a cigarette, my mom soon joined him at this point the police walked up and asked them "Are you two happy now? You have nothing left in the house! Looks like you two done some spring cleaning. Are you done yet? Because if you're not we have a problem!"

My dad finally said "Yes officer we're done, just had to blow off some steam. We are better now." "Good" the officer said "Now look at your boys standing in the road, embarrassed and ashamed. How do you think that makes them feel? Because if it were me I would feel pretty shitty, now get this mess cleaned up because when we come back and it's still here we take your boys and neither one of you will ever see them again".

For the next few months it seemed we were a happy family but I still had fears it would change again. My mom stepped around the corner and said "Bob, tomorrow is your birthday what kind of cake do you want and who do you want to invite?" I said "Chocolate and can I invite my friend Donnie?" and to my surprise she replied "Sure you can, go let him know ok."

So I rushed out the door before she could change her mind, ran all the way to his house "Hey, Donnie you want to come to my birthday party tomorrow?" and Donnie immediately said "Sure I do, it will be fun", "great you want to come down and play at my house? And he said "Nawww I have to stay here, my mom grounded me for the day". With that I told Donnie" Well got to run now, see you tomorrow ok" I was excited; I am getting a cake and my best friend is going to be there, I walked pretty fast back to the house and couldn't wait till my birthday night fall came and we were all sitting around the living room watching TV when my dad spoke up, "seems to me that someone needs to get in bed, I heard there will be birthday party tomorrow for a certain young man".

I didn't miss a beat; I took off out of the bedroom excited. I couldn't sleep a wink all night, I laid in bed watching for daylight to break over the trees here it comes day light oh yeah it's my birthday; it's my birthday. I jumped out of bed ran around the house it's my birthday. I'm eight years old today, wake up it's my day and my brother Gary rose up and said "Shut up Bob and go back to bed", my brother Jason threw his pillow at me and my mom and dad said "Bob get back into bed right now!"

I tipped toed into the kitchen hoping to catch a glimpse of my cake, I looked everywhere no cake. Sitting at the table wondering did my mom forget my cake? Or is she making it today? Yeah that's it, she is making it today.

I put on my clothes and my jacket and went outside it was November and cold but I didn't care, it was my birthday. It was about an hour before everyone else got up and my dad looked at me "Bob, you want to come to work with me today?" Sure dad lets go we loaded up the truck and off we went. As pulled into the work site, my dad said "Bob, now stay out of the way ok, you're not strong enough to lift those stones", wrong thing to say to me on my birthday! I was older now and stronger, boy was I wrong within an hour. My arms and back were screaming in pain but I didn't let it show, didn't want to disappoint my dad so I toughed it out.

By the end of the day I could hardly move but I was excited about my party and dad said "You worked hard today son, I was very proud of you." With smile and pride across my face I replied "Thanks dad".

We pulled into the driveway I jumped out of the truck, ran inside, no surprise, no happy birthday. My brothers were gone and my mom was sitting in the living room. With disappointment for not having a birthday party, I walked outside and saw David playing under the oak tree. I asked him if he would like to go explore the woods.

We ran as fast as we could to the woods "Hey Bob come here?" With a sound of fear in his voice. What's that with a bewildered look on his face I turned around and said "David don't move! Just stand still" The biggest snake I have ever seen in my life. "David slowly step towards me" as I put myself between him and the snake. I have always had a fascination with snakes.

David stepped behind me as I braced myself for the strike, "David back up and hand me that stick on the ground?" The snake coiled up and getting ready to strike locked on me. "David handed me the stick" I reached in with it and the snake grabbed to the stick, I pushed its head down and grabbed it by the back of its head.

"You got It" David said, I lifted it up half its body still laying on the ground "How did you do that?" David asked, "Pawpaw showed me how" "well Bob you can just keep that one to yourself, I don't want to know anything about catching snakes" I laughed "Ok not a problem David".

"What are you going to do with it? As David started backing away "Well I'm thinking about setting free in a few minutes", as he starting running away "Ok let it go" Laughing so hard I couldn't catch my breath, "Ok" I started unwrapping the snake from my arm and put its head under a small log and jumped about five feet backwards as it got free I looked up David was dust in the wind, he already blazed a trail through the woods like a rabbit.

You should have heard the feet running to the kitchen, we sounded like a herd of elephants it was time to take dad to the hospital for his surgery.

We loaded up in the car and off we went to the hospital as we pulled in my mom turn off the car and said "If anyone of you act like animals in here I swear to god you will not walk again."

When we finally got dad to his room we stayed for a little while. As we started to leave my dad cleared his throat and said "Bob, son come here for second?" So I walked to his bed and he said

"Debra take the other boys out for second". My dad looked at me and said "Son I know you are not the oldest but son you are going to have step up to the challenge". I knew what he was saying, I could also hear it in his voice, the fear I thought I would never hear in my dad.

I knew then something bad was wrong and a cold chill surrounded me. "Dad, are you ok?" I asked him he smiled and said "Yes of course" he hugged me and said "Now go home, you need to rest". He smiled and pushed me towards the door.

As we all got into the car I looked up at my dad's room window and he was standing at the glass with one hand touching the glass as if he knew that he would never see his family again.

That was the longest drive home I could remember. There wasn't a word spoken the whole way. The second we pulled into the driveway my mom told us everyone get in bed early, we have to be back at the hospital in the morning.

I don't think any of us slept that night, as the daylight came rolling in the next morning we all got dressed and went as fast as we could to hospital so we wouldn't miss dad before surgery.

My mom said "Ok boys, I have to make a stop on our way". We stopped off at a house in Eagleton Village were this man came out and gave my mom a hug and they went in, she was in there for almost two hours.

We missed my dad's time frame. When she came out I was so pissed off, I just wanted her to die. I hated my mother she was so selfish and so cold. As we approached the hospital I jumped out of car and started to run in the door David yelled "Bob wait for me, wait for me!" I took him by his hand and we went up stairs, it was too late; my dad was already in surgery. I looked at my mom with such hatred. As we waited for the doctor to let us know how dad was doing?

With sorrow and hunger my aunt went home and made food for everyone, as she left the doctor came in and said "Mrs. Jenkins, if we take his leg he will live a full life", my mom looked at the doctor. I said "That's great; I get to keep my dad!"

She told me to hush and she looked at the doctor and said "If you don't take the leg?"

The doctor looked at my mom "We will most likely lose him." She spoke in anger "I will not have him around my boys with one leg so do try again!"

The doctor looked at my mom with a stunned look on his face, he turned and looked right at me and dropped his head I knew right then my dad was not going to make it.

An hour went by and the doctor returns and said "I'm sorry he is gone, we did everything we could". I dropped to my knees and cried. David came over and leaned into me and cried. My mom took my brother Jason and held him and my brother Gary was with my aunt. The doctor came over to me and David and said "Come here young men? Walk with me", he took us into the hall and said "If there is anything I can help with please let me know?" I looked at him and said; I want my dad back and I ran to his room.

My dad was laying in his bed; he had so many wires hooked up to him. I saw his heart beat on the monitor and smiled so big; I knew it; I knew it, the doctor was lying, my dad was alive I reached out and took his hand in mine and it was ice cold. He never flinched and I said; "Dad wake up, please wake up?"

The doctor entered the room and knelt down beside me put his arm around me and said; "Son it's the machines keeping your dad alive, so if you have something you want to say now is the time to say it!" He stepped back and I leaned in and whispered in my dad's ear. "Dad if you can hear me I love you please don't go I need you here with me I have so much to learn and I need you to teach me."

As tears rolled down my face I let go of his hand and dropped to my knees and asked god to take care of my dad, he is the only dad I have and will ever have. Dear lord please keep my daddy safe let no more harm come to him. Give him happiness in heaven being that he didn't have it here, amen. As I turned to walk out of the room the doctor and nurse were standing there with tears in their eyes.

I walked out of the room and leaned against the wall and dropped down to the floor. The nurse walked out and reached down and took me in her arms and held me till I stopped crying. At that time my mom walked around the corner not a tear in her eye and said "Let's go boy time to go home."

It seemed like an eternity for us to get home. We turned the curve and pulled into our driveway this time it was so cold and lonely a million miles to our front door and it took my mom no time at all to find the bottle and put hell on earth for me and David.

For days my mom stayed drunk, I was just waiting for the beatings to start and it didn't take long for her to do just that. It was the first week of December and it was cold. There was no fire built so I got up to start one when I noticed mom was gone, nowhere to be seen. I thought well she is gone to get more beer. Little did I know it would take her two weeks to show back up.

I started a fire and David was still asleep I went to the refrigerator to see about making something for breakfast for us and there was nothing there! So I looked in the cabinets still nothing there.

We had no food, so I did the best I could to feed us. I worked around the neighborhood for money to buy food. Ten days went by and suddenly my mom shows up with this strange guy. I asked "Who is he? Her replied; "None of your damn business!"

As she continued to walk into the kitchen, she started cooking him the food I work so hard to get for me and David. I was mad, so I spoke out "Where have you been? why are you feeding him the food I got for me and David?"

She looked at me with anger in her eyes and said "You little son of a bitch! This is my house and what's in it is mine! If you don't like it, you can leave!" Without thinking I told her; "You're a sorry piece of trash." The next thing I knew I was getting knocked across the room.

David ran outside were that guy was sitting and drinking and he grabbed David and told him "Come here you little bastard". I got up and grabbed a hammer, ran outside and without thinking I hit him in the head and knock that sorry asshole out.

"Run David" I said in a whisper, "Hide in the bushes". Mom came out of the house with a rifle and aimed it right at me. I knew I was dead so I looked at her and said "go ahead bitch, shoot me, and go ahead kill me, like you did my dad!" She looked at me and smiled and said "You were a mistake anyway; no one will ever miss you!" She fired and hit me in the leg; I didn't even give her the pleasure of seeing me hurt.

As I lay on the ground bleeding, my mom said "Marvin lets go, I got us enough to eat and some money I found for beer". I tried to stop her from taking the food and money but I couldn't move. She walked by like nothing ever happened. When she and that son of a bitch left, David came out of the brush and ran up to help me to my feet and called our aunt to come help. As she was on her way I told David don't tell her what happened the family will get mad he said ok.

When my aunt showed up, she asked "What happened to you?" I told her I was playing with the rifle and it went off she looked at me like she knew I was lying. She looked at my leg and said it will be ok it just grazed you so she doctored my leg and asked "Where is your mother?" "Aunt Katherine, she is gone to the store she will be back in a few".

She said with such disbelief "OK" when she left David asked me "Why did you lie to her", and I held my head down and said if anyone finds out we are alone, the state will come take us away. He started crying I told him it's ok I won't let that happen I promise. He smiled and went to the kitchen and got him some water he came back and said "Bob there's no food!" I looked at him "I will get you something, just give me a few minutes and I will cook something".

I found some rice, "Wow, I never cooked rice before" but it was time for me to learn. David and I went into the kitchen and I said "OK" looking at the bag, mmmmmmmmmm here we go; that was the first time I have ever seen rice burn. I looked at David and smiled "Hey, let's have peanut butter and jelly sandwiches" he said awesome.

While he was eating I went in the bedroom and pulled thirty-five dollars I have saved for Christmas dinner and went back into the living room and said "David; how would you like to have hotdogs tonight for supper?" He said "that would be great", "Ok then, but you have to do me one favor, you need to help me learn my math problems?" So I created some math problems for him to learn.

When we were done working his math problems I said "You ready to go to the store and get those hotdogs?" With excitement in his eyes he said "Yes! Yes!" He jumped up grabbed mine and his skateboard and we took off to the store.

On our way we ran across Donnie; he was my best friend, "Hey guys were you going?" He asked we said "To the store" he said "Great, I will come along" on our way he said" You guys want to come to my house for dinner" a sigh of relief came over me "Sure if your mom don't care" he said "Come on".

So we went to his house, as we were waiting for his mom to finish cooking he asked David if he wanted to play ninja with him, David said sure so they went around back of the house and next thing I knew I heard David screaming.

Donnie had him on the ground choking him and calling him a little bastard. I ran and tackled Donnie and told him "You piece of shit, what are doing to my brother?" He laughed and said; it doesn't matter, his just a punk anyway. Well that didn't sit right with me so I ran towards Donnie took him to the ground, and continued to beat the shit out of him. I told him "Blood is thicker than friendship".

So I took a swing set chain and wrapped his arms and legs in it and dragged him in front of all the kids in the yard, told them "Look what I caught? A fish in a net" They laughed so hard, I took David by the hand and as we were walking away Donnie's mother screamed out "Don't ever come back!"

Their neighbor, which was an elderly man walked to his fence and said "Hey young man come here a second?" I thought to myself oh no, he is going to be mean to us also. We walked over and said

"Here son, here is twenty dollars for whipping that little punks butt, he has tortured my dog for months and I enjoyed the show, I wanted to pay you for it". He laughed as he walked away. I felt bad for what I had done to Donnie but David was my responsibility and I took that very serious.

As we got to the store, Mr. Arwood looked down at us and said "Well, well, well, if it isn't the pistol creek boys, how you young men doing today?" We smiled and said "We are great sir how are you?" He smiled and looked over at a customer and said so polite "This young man, but I will tell you this young man will be something big one day!" I thought he was talking about my weight so I told him; "Well, we would of like four hotdogs, but I don't want to be big so, can you just give David two" and he laughed.

The customer laughed as I was standing there wondering what they were laughing at. He said "Bobby, you will never reach my size, I'm so fat nothing grows in the shade" I didn't know what that meant till I got older. "Tell you what son, I have some clean up in the back for you to do if you take care of that I will give you six hotdogs and a couple of sodas" and of course my reply was "Yes sir". I ran to the back where his wife was working and said "Ma'am, your husband sent me back to help you with this if you like I will do this for you?" She smiled and said "Well thank you and I would like the break". So I continued to sweep, mop and stack until it was all done. We ate like kings that day.

The sun started to set on the river as we rode our skate boards along, as we approached the house we saw the electric company pulling away, we walked in and the power has been turned off.

Worried and didn't know what to do, it was cold and that house was scary at night. So I went to the meter base and studied it for a bit, I took the cover off the meter and trimmed two pieces of copper wire and took my life in my own hands and wala power! We stayed up till about midnight and fell asleep watching Johnny Carson.

The next morning it was freezing cold so I started a fire so David wouldn't be cold, I made both of us oatmeal to eat. As he woke up and came into the kitchen and said "What are we going to do today?" I told him "We were going to clean house first, then go to the park." With excitement in his eyes he started cleaning.

Later that morning we hear a car pull up and it was the police, so I grabbed David and we went to the back of the house and didn't make a sound. The policeman knocked several times and walked around the house looking in the windows, hiding in the corner of the closet I told David "sssshhhhhh he is here to take us away". David grabbed my arm and said "OK" and he was shaking as we heard the car drive off. I told David "Tag, your it! Catch me if you can?" He chased me around the house laughing. I had to get his mind off of what just happened.

David asked "Are we still going to the park"? I said "No, we are going to find us a Christmas tree" He said "Oh yeah" I figured if we were in the woods they would never find us, so I went to wood shed and got an axe and off we went we searched for hours. There were plenty to cut but just didn't want to go home too soon, so when the sun started to set I found one to cut. After I cut it down, David and I carried it to the house. It was a small tree but all we could carry; we didn't have any decorations so we were going to make some out of paper.

That night we sat down and started cutting the paper and coloring the Christmas decorations, colors all over the place. I went outside and pulled some leaves from the yard and told David to come out back, I had went to the shed and pulled out some spray paint and decided to color some of the leaves to hang on the tree.

It wasn't the prettiest tree in the world, but it was ours. You could see the pride busting out of David eyes like he just won a million dollars. I told David "Wow, you did an awesome job on the tree little bro, you should be proud!"

He looked at me and said "We have done an awesome job! You helped", "ok, we done an awesome job!" I replied.

After a few I asked "David would you like some snow cream?" immediately his reply was "Oh yeah". There wasn't any snow on the ground, but we had plenty of ice shavings in the freezer, so I went and got the vanilla flavoring and sugar and cinnamon, it wasn't the best in the world but it would do.

As the evening came closer David looked at me and said "Are we going to be ok? Bob are we going to be ok?" At that very moment he said something to me that changed me for the rest of my life.

He got silent for a second and smiled saying "Of course we will, you will make sure of it. You are the older brother and I know you will make it ok".

From that day on my childhood died and adult hood stepped up and took control.

I realized at that moment I had a baby brother to take care of in every way. I would not let him down for nothing, looking at David with a firm look on my face I told him "I will not let anything happen to you period! I will take care of you, I promise! Now let's get some rest we have a big day ahead of us tomorrow".

That night we heard a noise coming from the back room, David pulled the cover over his head as I got up and went to the back bedroom door and all of a sudden I heard; crash, the sound of breaking glass rang out.

I ran to the closet and got the shot gun, I pushed the door open and there in the window was two legs crawling in, I fired! The legs weren't there anymore, from the other room I heard David screaming. Ran in there and said "David are you ok"? He jumped up and said "What was that? I said

"it was just a mouse and I blew it away". He said "Oh ok good! So we can go to sleep now?" I said yes, he slept all that night while I stayed up keeping an eye on things.

The next morning seemed like everything started getting better, it was a beautiful day and for some reason it seemed different. David got out of bed and said "Today I am going to cook for you", so here we go, hurricane David and a bag of flour . . . oh wow it looked like a blizzard hit the kitchen.

When he was done I saw the biggest, ugliest breakfast I have ever seen. I think I said two prayers, one for him to be ok and one for me to survive this living breathing breakfast that he called pancakes. I swear I thought it had a pulse.

After living through breakfast I looked at David and asked "Hey, do you want to work on a science project with me" His reply was "I'm not feeling well today"

I took his temperature, he had a fever of 102 degrees, so I put him back to bed and we stayed in the whole day, I doctored him all day and night.

"Wake up David let's take your temperature and see if you are better today"? David tossed the blanket over his head and I said to him "Two days till Christmas, we have to get you better so Santa won't be afraid to come in the house" He turned over and said "oh alright".

He rose up like he was dead, tired but thank god he didn't have a fever so I told him "Hey, let's do something fun today! Lets figure out what we want to do for each other for Christmas?" He said "OK".

So he went running into the bedroom and shut and locked the door, he was in there for almost three hours. I went outside where I was building a bicycle for myself in the work shop and I thought to myself I will build this for David!

I was missing one wheel, a chain and a seat. I already put bearings and forks on it and it hit me; I saw an old bike at the old ladies house up the street. I went to David and said "I will be right back!"

So I went next door and asked Shelia if she would come over and keep an eye on David. Shelia was a very pretty Indian girl that I liked. I wanted to be her boyfriend but was too shy to ask! She said "Sure no problem". So off I went to the ladies house, I walked up to the house and asked the older of the two "I noticed you had an old bike in your wood bin and I'm trying to build my little brother a bike for Christmas, and I need that bike for parts. Is there any way I could work for payment for the bike"?

She looked up and put her finger on her cheek and said "Why yes, yes there is young man! Come with me", she said and led me to the back of the house where there was a stack of wood to bust for her fire place, "If you will bust all that wood to fit in my fire place I will give you that bike". I looked at the wood and said to myself; oh my god she must off had the forest brought in but I was determined to get that bike ready for David. So I grabbed the axe and started splitting wood by the time I got half way done I had blisters on my hands and wow did they hurt.

When I finished the job three hours later, I went to lady and said "Ma'am I'm done". Now she said "That's great but could you bring me enough inside to last till morning"? God I wanted to say no, but I couldn't, she was kind enough to give me work to earn that bike so I said yes. Off I went carrying wood inside for her and her sister. When I went inside, her sister was lying on a bed that looked like my dad's bed in the hospital; she sat down beside her bed and started telling me about their childhood together.

How they always stayed by each other's side and took care of one another, she looked at me and smiled and said I know what you're going through young man and I am so sorry for how your mother has done you! Stand by your brother; be there for him because one day he will be gone.

I looked at the lady and said "Ma'am my name is Bobby and if you wouldn't mind I would like to stop in from time to time and check on both of you"?

She smiled "We would like that very much Bobby and thank you"! I said "I have to go now, and she did not forget to give me the bike and also handed me a fruit cake, I hate fruit cake but I didn't let her know that.

I went to the wood bin and got the bike and I ran all the way home slipped it into the shed and went inside and told Shelia "Thank you and I'm sorry it took so long", she said "That it fine, by the way where is your mom?"

I hated lying to her so I told her; she was at the hospital getting medicine for David. She was satisfied with my response. I told her what I was doing for David's Christmas present and she said "Hey, can I help?" I responded "Sure" so we both went to the shed and opened the door and turned to let her go in first and she kissed me! WOW, I was in heaven, but first thing first, we started working on the bike and I don't think I worked a second on that bike without having a smile on my face. Yeap, you guessed it! It was the kiss come on I'm a guy duh.

After about thirty minutes I could hear her dad yelling for her she had to go, at that instant she kissed me again and said bye and she ran home. I continued to work on the bike.

Around six o'clock I went in to cook dinner and to my surprise Shelia already made us sandwiches and soup.

When we sat down at the table I asked David "So what have you been doing today? He giggled and said "Aawww, nothing" "Come on David, what have you been doing? Once again his reply was "Nothing".

After we finished dinner, I wrote Shelia a note and slipped in her mail box.

I went back to work on the bike, Christmas was two days away. Around ten o'clock, it was finished and I went inside. David was sitting in the living room floor coloring, he said "Bob, go away go away! I'm working on your Christmas present". So I told him that I would be in the kitchen if you need me and so I walked away smiling.

That night as we laid down and David said in a soft voice "Tomorrow is Christmas evening and I can't wait". "David the sooner you go to sleep the sooner it will get here" I said. I don't think neither one of us slept that night, as the morning came rising over the trees, we both got up and it was Christmas Eve.

I fixed David some breakfast and he walked into the kitchen and said "Merry Christmas". He had news paper for wrapping and duct tape to hold it together and it was the best present I could have ever gotten. As I un-wrapped it, he sat with the biggest smile on his face. "WOW, I have always wanted this" I said to my baby brother! The present was three pennies and four marbles, he said "Do you really like it", and I said that I love it.

I have always wanted to play marble pennies so I quickly invented a game, I laid all three pennies on the floor and flipped the marbles at them making the marbles jump off the floor and acted like it was the most fun I could ever have. He then handed me the picture he colored, it was of me and him. I got up and walked towards the door with tears in my eyes and he asked "Where you going?" I told him I was going to get his present so stay inside ok? He said "YEEAAAAAAA, ok"

I went to the building wiped away my tears and got control of myself and took the bike from the building and set it outside the kitchen door, went back inside and said "David, no peaking now". He almost knocked me down running past me turned into the kitchen and said "Where is it? Where is it?" I laughed and said "It's outside the door", he ran to door opened it and WOW, WOW, WOW.

He turned and ran to me hugging me. We grabbed our coats and told him I'm going to teach you how to ride the bike.

We walked down to the park where the sidewalks were and David jumped on his bike and said "Come on Bob, push me, come on, come on". I walk up behind him and slowly walked beside him with my hand on the seat I told him" Peddle David you can do it!"

He started smiling and I thought for sure he had it, at that moment I saw him rolling towards the creek "David, hit the brakes! HIT the brakes!" I screamed

He screamed and suddenly he disappeared, went right off the bank into the creek bed, I ran down to the edge of the bank and there he was sitting in the creek, laughing. I stood up straight and asked him "Are you ok," he just looked at me and said "Yes". I knew he would catch pneumonia if I didn't get him out of those wet clothes so I took him wrapped him in my jacket and took him home.

I ran him a hot bath and got him some dry clothes, while he undressed and got into the tub I pulled the door to just enough to keep an eye on him. As he was bathing I cooked him some tomato soup and crackers.

"Bob" he yelled out, "I'm ready" so I took a towel and dried him off. He said "Where is the bike?" I told him it was in the shed and that I had to do some work on it. The next day was Christmas so David and I went to bed early.

The next morning it was freezing so I got up and thought I could just put some fire starter fluid into the fire place, so I soaked the wood and struck a match and tossed in the wood. Suddenly it exploded into face, I was burning, I was screaming, flames everywhere "OH MY GOD, HELP ME, HELP ME" I went running into the kitchen not knowing any better and ran water over my head, it just made it worse. My face was burning, my jacket was on fire. I ran into the living room dropped to floor tried everything I could. David came running with his jacket and tossed it over my head and the flames were gone.

But the pain remained, oh god it hurts, it hurts so bad. Help me, help me. I ran outside screaming David called my aunt she called our mom which was less than a mile away.

She came rushing home not because she was scared about what happened to me, but because she knew if she didn't she would end up in jail. In shock and scared and still in so much pain, my mother told me shut up before you get me pulled over I have been drinking and can't afford to go to jail.

Driving to the hospital my mom kept telling me "If I go to jail because of this I will hurt you boy"

god how I wanted to tell them about my mom but I couldn't I would lose David and that will never happen. Pulling into the emergency room drop off I jumped out of the car and ran into the waiting room, where an orderly was standing. He took one look at me and said "Come with me son" he told my mom she needed to fill out some paper work.

When she was done to come back to my room and she asked "What did you tell them? What did they ask?" I looked at her and said nothing.

The orderly walked in and my mom was so nervous she didn't say a word he started putting cold cream on my burns and god it did hurt I started crying and the orderly looked at me and said "If you don't stop fighting me I will stop putting this on you!"

The nurse was standing in the door way and told the orderly that he needed to leave right now, she came over, knelt down beside me and said "Hey cutie, would you please stop crying for me I promise I won't hurt you!" I saw kindness in her eyes so she began to wrap my head with gauze, she talked to me as she wrapped. She asked me if I played sports, I said yes baseball and she smiled with excitement in her voice and turned to mother and said "Wow, a baseball player bet your really good too aren't you?" before I knew it she was done and left the room.

As I started to rise from the bed, the doctor came and said we need to unwrap him so I can look at the scaring; she looked at me with concern and said "I need you to be a big boy for me ok?"

I knew right then I was going to hurt I felt every inch of the gauze as they pulled it off my face god how it hurt. The tears flowed, but I didn't make a sound, I didn't want to make anyone else mad at me so I remembered what my dad use to tell me "Suck it up, the pain it only hurts for a minute." No disrespect to my dad, but that was so not true".

When the doctor was done they wrapped me back up and looked at my mom and said "We would like to keep him over night to keep an eye on him?" My mom told the doctor that she was a certified nurse's aide and knew what to do and she would keep an eye on me.

I looked at my mom, I knew she wouldn't do it but I kept my mouth shut and played the loving son when we got home my mom said "You boys go back in the house I will be right back".

David helped me in the house, I laid down on the sofa and David asked "You need anything" I said "I'm fine David" So he sat on the sofa below my feet the whole time three hours went by, as we waited for mom to come back. It never happened; she didn't come back so David and I fell asleep on the sofa.

The next morning I woke up and there was my brother Gary, he was crying with a hand on my leg, I looked at him and asked "Are you ok? Is something wrong?" And he laughed and said "Is something wrong? Yes, something is wrong! What happened to you?" I told him what had happened and he looked at the ground then looked up and said "Guys, I'm so sorry I would take you with me but we just don't have the room" I said with sadness in my heart "it's ok I understand".

He stood up and said; "I have to go now" and walked out the door. Me and David walked over to the window and watched him drive away; it was like no one wanted us? What was so wrong with us, that no one in our family wanted us? We were good kids, we didn't cause problems. We watched Gary drive away.

David said "Bob you lay down, it's my turn to take care of you!" I looked at David with a smile and said "David we will take care of each other." So we began cleaning up the mess and I tossed the curtains in the garbage I got the mop and broom, "Bob I will start sweeping" he said.

After we were done cleaning my face started hurting and bleeding, it was time to clean and change the bandages I remembered what the doctor said twice a day for a month.

I sat down on the sofa and had David hold a mirror for me while I started un-wrapping the gauze. God it hurt with every turn when I got down to the gauze pads, I stopped wondering what I was going to look like. Was I going to be a monster? Was I ever going to be the same look the same? "David" I said with concern for him "You don't have to look if you don't want to".

David looked at me and said these words to me I will never forget, "Bob I don't care what you look like you will always be my brother", that told me at that moment that nothing will ever separate us.

I slowly removed each gauze and each time pain took over my body David started crying I asked "If you can't stand to look at me I will understand if you want to leave?" "No!" He said "It's not that it's that I hate seeing you hurt".

55

It was time for me to see the monster I created, David held up the mirror and I started crying that wasn't me in the mirror, my face swollen and disfigured. The blood and fluid I started crying harder it hurt as each tear rolled down my raw skin. David put his arm around me and said "Bob it will go away and you will look just fine".

I thought to myself; school will be starting back soon, what am I going to do? People will make fun of me, call me names; the air started hitting my burns so I started to put the cold cream on my face, wow it felt so good but hurt a little.

When I was done with the cold cream David asked "Can I wrap you back up?" I wished I could have smiled but it hurt "David you can help me wrap it up".

With each gauze I told David here hold the end so I could clamp it into place, when were done I looked at David "Hey, want to watch some football? The Redskins play today." He started laughing and said "You look like a Redskin with your bandage off." I laughed, god it hurt but I laughed. The cowboys and Redskins were going into the fourth quarter. David had fallen asleep and I could feel my face throbbing so I got up and took my medicine, not the full dosage the doctor said. I had to stay awake in case David woke up, so I sat down and began to write poetry. I remember the first poem I ever wrote;

> "Sad and confused
> Lost and alone how I wished to god
> I was older and grown,
> My childhood gone like the summers day.
> Gone from this life my childhood days".

David woke up yelling my name, I ran into the living room "I'm right here David, are you ok?" he said "I had a bad dream Bob. I dreamed you were gone and left me all alone." I looked at him and told him "That would never happen", he rubbed his eyes and said "Ok, good because it's just us Bob, we have to stick together and take care of each other".

A few days went by it was almost time to go back to school, I was so afraid the other kids would make fun of me. On the first day of school, I walked David to school and ran back home before anyone could see me, I was so afraid people would laugh at me, call me names.

When I got home, I ran inside and locked the door. I never went outside or showed my face.

I would sit and do math problems, read a book or challenge myself with spelling words, I thought that way I could still learn and not get into trouble. When it was time to pick up David I would have him meet me in the wooded lot next to the school so no one would see me. "How was your day David" he said "It was good, the teachers were asking me were you were at". "And what did you tell them David?" "I told them you were sick."

That went on for almost two weeks, then one day my teacher showed up at the house, her name was Mrs. Barnett I love that lady. She was my favorite teacher, she knocked on the door and I answered; "Yes, may I help you?" she replied: "Bob is that you? Are you ok? Can I come in?" Nervous and scared I said "Yes, come in."

Mrs. Barnett asked "How you are feeling?" She saw my bandages and asked "Oh my lord, what happened?" I started crying and told her about catching myself on fire, she reached out and took me in her arms and "Oh my god, baby you will be ok". After about an hour she looked at me with a smile and said "Come to school tomorrow and I will keep you in my class all day and no one will make fun of you if they do I will take care of it."

The next day I walked with David to school, the kids all stared at me, pointing, some asked "What happened, are you ok?", and I said "Yeah just want to go to class". As I approached my classroom the math teacher Mr. Dotson looked at me and said "It's about time you get back to school, maybe you might just pull off being smarter". I hated that man he was such a bastard.

Sitting in class was so hard, everyone looking and whispering the bell rang it was lunch time, everyone walked out of the room but me! Mrs. Barnett looked at me and said "Come here I have lunch for us" I was ashamed and embarrassed because I couldn't afford lunch money I was saving it for David.

"Thank you" she smiled and said "It's ok. I couldn't of ate it all so thank you for keeping me from wasting, would you like to go outside for a while and exercise?" and my reply was "No thank you ma'am", "alright" she said," Whenever you're ready just let me know ok".

E. B. Johnston

The end of the school day was approaching, I was eager to get it over with. The bell sounded I grabbed my things and ran out the side door searching for David, I had so many kids staring at me and it was so uncomfortable. At that moment I saw my brother David off in a distance, he was running towards the gate and there were two boys chasing him.

I darted like a jack rabbit trying to get to him, when I finally caught up, the two boys had David cornered at the stop sign. That's it I thought to myself, so dropped my books and charged into them wreck less and uncaring, I yelled "Hey, you son of a bitches, leave my brother alone." I drew back and slammed the biggest one right in the mouth, he dropped like a rock in the water and the second one I turned and kicked him right in the balls, he bent over and kneed him right in the face.

I turned to David and said "Now stand up for yourself, fight back! Never run, never run again, be strong, be tough". He dropped his books with tears in his eyes I continued my lecture, "David toughen up, kick their asses!" At that moment, David screamed out like a rage of anger, and he started pounded the crap out of that guy.

I started stomping the bigger guy, the kids gathering around cheering us on, at that moment I looked up there was the teacher coming I told David "Run, don't get caught" he took off and the teacher grabbed me and said "What's going on here?" The other kids started saying they were ganging up on Bobby and he was defending himself.

Shocked and confused I stood there in silence, what just happened! I thought but one of the smaller kids said to me "We have your back Bob, don't worry". I smiled and one of them said to me "We will go with you" as we walked towards the school a group of kids followed.

The teacher turned and said "Go home son, we don't need to do this". It hit me; David was alone, I ran home he was sitting on the porch I sat down beside him in silence he looked at me and asked "Why did we have to fight?" I sat there for a moment in silence and replied, "We fight because we have too, not because we want too. It's not a friendly world we live in, sometimes we have to speak with our fists if our words don't help, never fight, never, never fight unless you have too and don't ever start a fight".

"I don't understand" David said with a confused look on his face, and I explained "It's like this, if you can get out of fighting by talking it out, that's great but sometimes people just won't talk so you have to defend yourself. By the way why were those guys chasing you?" and his reply was "They were making fun of you and I called them stupid" I dropped my head I never thought how it would affect David, "I'm sorry it's my fault I will make it better".

The next day I went to school, walked up to both of those guys and said "Hey, I heard you guys were making fun of me and my brother was having to listen to what you said and he defended me and both of you felt you should make his life a living hell. Well here I am, make fun of me, go ahead I'm a big boy and I can take it.

But let me say this first if either one of you ever pick on my brother again, I will get my friends to make sure both of you will have to run home every day for the rest of your life!, So here I am, let's hear it, come on", they stood there in silence and I took it a little further I grabbed the bandages on my head and started pulling them off, "Here, you want to see what you were laughing at" I pulled so hard it started bleeding. The boys looked at me in disbelief. "Oh my god", one of them said we didn't know it was that.

At that moment Mrs. Barnett walked up and saw my face and she started crying and said "Come with me Bob" and proceeded to take me to the nurse's office. The nurse re-wrapped my face. They both looked at me and said, "Why did you un-wrap your face?" And I told them, "Those two boys were being mean to my brother and I wanted them to see why".

Both Mrs. Barnett and the nurse sat down and looked at each other and started talking. The nurse turned and said "You know that was a pretty brave young man and I need help in here today would you mind sticking around?" I said with excitement "sure" I have never seen what she does here.

Mrs. Barnett went to the principal and asked if she could leave for a moment and if he would cover for her and he said of course. She turned to me and smiled; when she came back she had David with her, "how would you and David like to come with me tomorrow after school? Only with your mother's permission of course".

Looking at her I said "Ok, I will bring you a note from my mom" and she smiled and said "Of course" When the school day ended David and I walked home excited about tomorrow. "What do you think it's about Bob?" I said "I don't know but it's going to be awesome".

That night it hit me, she knows about mom not being home, I can't let us be separated. She is going to put us in separate homes and that can't happen. So the next morning I got up and turned the alarm clock off and when David woke up it was too late to go to school.

"What happened? Why didn't the alarm go off? We are supposed to go with your teacher today". I looked at David and told him "I don't know, the power must have gone off thru out the night".

We sat around all day, wondering what it was she had planned for us. We soon found out. She pulled up in the driveway with bags in her arms she left them on the door step with a note that said "Just wanted to give the boys a special little something, I noticed their coats were worn out with holes in them and the lining was coming undone. Hope I didn't cross the boundaries just care. Have a nice day and thank you Mrs. Judy Barnett".

My heart dropped, I handed David his coat and took mine into the bedroom. I cried in shame of myself, I felt like I disappointed her. She is one of the reason I have a heart to this very day and I will carry only the greatest memories of her for the rest of my life.

Looking down the hall I could see David modeling his new jacket like it was gold, I whispered to myself thank you Mrs. Barnett you are the best. We couldn't wait to go outside and try our new coats as we started to go out, my brother Jason pulled up and looked at me and David and said "Hey guys meet Sonya" and we replied "Hello Sonya", she replied "It's nice to meet you and David". With that I and David went out to play for a while.

After a bit Sonya asked if we would like some spaghetti. "Awesome it's been a long time since we had that and thank you" we said and off we went to play in the woods. We found a couple of sticks that looked like rifles and played soldiers I buried myself in leaves as David tried to sneak by, I raised up and he about jumped out of his skin "Bang, bang, I got you" and he pretended to be shot.

He dropped to his knees and groaned rolled down the hill stood up leaned against a tree and said "Oh, you got me" and dropped to his knees again looked up and said "Oh, awwwww, "Oh" I said "Come on, die already" he smiled and "Fooled you". "You missed and shot me" I dropped to my knees and said "Oh you got me" and continued to die a horrible long glorious death as he leaned up against a tree started whistling and said "Are you done yet?"

We both laughed, I looked at him "I'm going to get you David" and he took off like a rabbit, I chased him all over that hill side, we fell down "I'm getting hungry" he said smiling at me, so we started walking home as we approached the house we could smell the food and took off running into the house.

I told David go wash your hands as I went into the kitchen. I stood by the stove looking at Sonya and said "It smells good" I leaned over and said; "Wow, those noodles look like worms!" Before I knew it Jason grabbed me by my hair and pushed me into the wall then proceeded to grabbed my throat and said "You little son of bitch, she is nice enough to cook for you and you bad mouth her food?" I couldn't breathe tears rolling from my eyes and fear throughout my body.

He turned me loose, grabbed me by my hair again, pushed me in front of Sonya and said "Tell her you're sorry" I looked up at her crying and said "I'm sorry, I didn't mean anything by it".

He turned me loose and said "Since you don't like worms, you don't eat! How's that!"

Sonya looked at him and said "It's ok, he was kidding" Jason looked at her and said "No, it's not ok" he dragged me to my room by my shirt and said "While we eat you stay in here". Hungry and scared I stayed in my room until he came to get me an hour later and said they were leaving and maybe next time I be nicer. As they left I locked my door and started crying.

David stood outside my door and said "Bob I have something for you", he got seconds of the food and put it in the oven for me and said "I have food for you Bob". I bolted out of the room and took the food out of the oven and said "Thanks David" and he said "You're welcome"

At this time David and I went into the living room and said "By the way they took the TV what are we going to do?" We had a old TV in storage with no sound and a radio in my room, so I took the back off the TV, stripped the wires to the speaker and wired it into the radio, so we could have sound. I watched my dad do the same thing to a car speaker to TV he had in his work shop.

For the next three months it was pretty normal David and myself. Pretty much took care of one another, but the day came my bandages was to come off my face, since mom wasn't around I figured I would just take them off myself. So one morning I said to David "Are you ready for this to come off my head" and he looked and smiled "Yeah, let's do it".

Scared of what I might look like, I started slowly removing the gauze. Finally it was gone and David standing there with a concerned look on his face, "What is it David? Do I look bad? Am I a monster?" His reply was "Hey Bob, I hate to tell you this" as I look into the mirror he says "Ugly, you have always been ugly" and laughed. I was me again "No scars" and David started laughing harder. I got up and said to him "I'm going to get you" chasing him out the door and up the street and we both stopped running. Off in the distance we saw our mom's car heading our way.

"Hide" I yelled out to David here she comes as we both darted for the bushes. As she went by we noticed she wasn't alone, we started slowly heading back to house and we knew she was up to something. We waited for her to go into the house and at that moment she started yelling "Boys are you here? Come here I have something to tell you".

I looked at David "Let's go see what she wants". As we started walking towards the house, fear in both our faces as she stepped out of the front door, "Boys, there you are! Come here babies, mama has something to tell you" we sat down on the steps as she went on about how she met someone and got married to a guy named Marvin, and how they were going to Florida for their honeymoon.

"So we wanted to spend some time with you guys before we leave". I thought to myself if we go with them for a little awhile maybe she will leave and not come back. "So, I said sure" and loaded up in the car and went to my aunt's house. There my mom asked my aunt if she would keep an eye on David for one night while she and Marvin took me camping to get to know him.

So David stayed at my aunt's house, mom and me went and picked Marvin up. As he got in the car he looked at me and smiled and said "No hard feelings about the hammer thing ok little man!"

I looked confused and said "OK", we took off for the camping ground. I was excited and nervous, the thought of maybe they we're going to kill me did entered my mind, but I didn't care, I was pretty much over this life.

As we pulled into the campsite I noticed there were no other campers or houses for miles. I was alone with them and if I knew what was coming I would have never gotten in that car. Marvin looked at me and said "Hey Bob come help me unload the car so I can set up the tents and campsite", "Sure, no problem" I replied, I walked over and grabbed the fire wood.

Marvin smiled and said "You're pretty strong for a little guy!" My mom said; "Yes he is! All my boys are strong". As we continued to unload Marvin said "Hey why don't you take this rod and reel and go catch dinner. I thought to myself; maybe this guy wasn't so bad after all. I smiled and said "Ok not a problem" As I walked towards the lake, I could hear my mom say we need to be careful or this could get very ugly! I didn't realize till later what she meant by that.

I thought she was talking about the rain coming in. It was getting late and the sun was setting and the rain clouds were coming over the mountains, as I walked back to camp I held up the seven fish and smiled "Here is dinner"; with pride on my face, Marvin said great come here I will show you how to clean them.

"I already know how to clean fish Marvin, just get the fire ready before it rains" he smiled saying "Ok little man you got it. Bring the fish to me when you get them cleaned!" "Ok" I replied with a smile on my face. As Marvin was cooking I looked over and my tent wasn't put up, "Why isn't my tent set up" I asked, Marvin looked at my mom and said "We couldn't find the hardware Bob" My mom spoke up, "guess you will have to share our tent with us". I said "Nawwww, that's ok I will find my hardware and set it up", so I began searching. I knew I had the hardware with my tent I always keep it in the same bag.

Dinner was ready and it was starting to rain, we ate and laughed and cut up under the tree the rain started getting harder so they went into their tent and said "You can come join us if you want to Bob?", "No" I replied as I stood in the rain. I walked over to the car tried to get in but it was locked, so I went over and tossed my tent over my head, crouched down under the tree.

The rain started getting harder, it has been about three hours since they went in, so thought to myself; they are asleep so maybe I can sneak in and they won't know. So I slowly walked into the tent and lay in the far corner balled up and wet and cold scared of what might happen.

The night got longer and it got colder, my mom reached over and tossed a blanket on me it was so warm. About an hour went by and suddenly I felt a hand touching my shoulder and it slowly started rubbing my arm, I was so scared, fear rushed through my body as I was frozen and didn't know what to do. What to think and shaking, I'm so scared I could feel the hair on his arm touching my skin I started to have tears in my eyes. His hand moving down the side of my leg, in which locked together motionless. I couldn't move; oh god, what am I going to do I thought.

He slid his hand down on my over my penis and I couldn't breathe; run that's all I could think of, just get up and ran. Would he chase me? Would he kill me? And leave me in the woods? So many thoughts, so many fears I didn't know what to do or where to go.

I screamed "Help! Someone help me!" As I bolted out of the tent running into the woods, and I thought to myself it's dark and maybe he can't find me.

I ran and ran, running into branches falling down, scared and wondering if I was going to die or if I would ever get to see David again and at that moment I realized this could have been David and that wasn't going to happen. Not to me and not to him, so ran faster until I came up on the main road and I knew where I was and a sigh of relief came over me.

Across the street was a grave yard, so I ran to the biggest grave stone I could find and hid behind it. Off in the distance I could see headlights so I started to run again, my aunt's house was just a mile or so up the road. Exhausted, wet and cold I started running again I thought for sure they were going after David I couldn't let that happen for nothing.

As I approached the house my aunt, my mom, my uncle and Marvin were standing in the porch, "There he is" my mom said "We were worried sick about you!, why did you bolt off into the woods like that?" She walked up and whispered in my ear "If you say a word you will not live to regret it"

I wanted to tell my aunt and uncle so bad what happened but the fear of something happening to me and not being able protect

David so I didn't say anything. My mom walked back on the porch gripping my arm so tight I lost the feeling in it. David walked out and said "Bob I'm mad at you! You got to go camping and I didn't" Marvin bent over and looked at David "We are going back there would you like to go?" I spoke up and said "No David please, I will stay here with you and we will explore the woods together you would like that?"

He said; "I want to go camping" I continued to tell David not to go, the water is muddy and the ground is soaked. You won't have any fun. My aunt looked at me with concern in her eyes and said "Naaaww, the boys can stay with us for awhile" and a world of fear left my body. My mom looked nervous as she walked off the porch and said maybe next time David.

My aunt said "Debra, wait a second?" as my aunt approached my mom and my mom looked at Marvin and said "Wait for me in the car, I will be right there" As he walked away he looked up at me standing on the porch and smiled and said "You take care little man I will be back to visit later". The fear returned as quickly as it left, I'm going to die! His going to kill me! I just know it, I grabbed David and looked Marvin in the eyes and said "Not if I visit you first!"

*To this day I still don't know why I said that. Mom and aunt were arguing at the foot of the steps, when my mom looked up at us and said "I will see you boys later" and she continued to walk to the car. She got in and as they drove away I ran down to the street so I could make sure they left. My aunt yelled "Bob come inside sweetheart, I bet you're hungry?" Wow food I thought to myself.*

*So I ran up the steps straight to bathroom to wash my hands and looked in the mirror, and broke down crying. I sat on the toilet barely catching my breath and my aunt came to the door and said "What's wrong? Are you ok?" I said "Yes Aunt Cathleen I'm ok". She asked if I could let her in and I replied "No, I wanted a few minutes just want to be alone".*

*She went and got my uncle, he spoke through the door "Boy are ok? Let me in? What's wrong?" I sat there wondering if they would believe me or if I should even tell. I decided not to say a word, it would it cause more harm than good. So I opened the door and told them I hurt my foot running up the steps. I could see it in my aunt's eyes she didn't believe me but she didn't push the issue. "Then let's eat, I bet you're hungry?" she said with a smile on her face as we went into the kitchen to carry the food into the dining room.*

We all sat down to eat, me, David, my aunt Cathleen my uncle Bud, my cousins; Eugene, Mary, Kim and Ramona. I looked at the food but I couldn't eat for some reason my aunt looked at me again and said "Bob come with me and let's talk?" We left the table and went into the living room. "Now tell me sweetheart, what happened at the lake" at this point I broke down crying and wrapped my arms around her. I can't tell you please, don't make me; I don't want to talk about it. she hugged me and said ok, when you're ready, ok just when you're ready I looked up at her caring and kind eyes and said one day ok I will I promise.

My aunt looked at me smiling and hugged me, "So what would you like to do today? You name it!" I looked at her and said I'm so sleepy I just want to go lay down with a hug she said "You go on upstairs and sleep", I jumped up and walked upstairs and laid down on the bed.

I was having such a bad dream about being raped and killed that I woke up I was soaking in sweat and screaming out. My aunt and uncle came running upstairs "Are you ok? What's wrong?" At this moment I could see the anger building in my uncle's eyes, "What happened to you at the lake? Talk to me boy right now?"

My aunt pushed him out of the room, "Bud calm down let me talk to him", and she said "Just go downstairs I will handle this".

Come here she said in a calming voice and pulled me in close, "Talk to me baby, tell me, I hate seeing you this way?" I told her what happened and she started crying and left the room I overheard her tell my uncle. At this time my uncle came in the room and asked which way they said they were going, tell me and I will fix this for you. If I told him he would have killed both of them so I just looked to the floor and said I don't know.

All night I sat by the window and wondered what I did for them to try to hurt me that way, after that day I was never the same. Again my heart grew cold and I never trusted anyone with David or my safety again. I was bitter towards the world and everyone in it.

Three weeks went by and I was in the barn helping my uncle with his cattle, when my brother Jason turned the corner and said "Hi guys what you all doing?" My uncle looked up and said "Hey there what have you been up to?", "Not much" he replied.

"Hey Bud can I speak to you a minute outside please?" "Sure" he said and walked outside as I was preparing the cows for auction.

Uncle Bud came back in the barn and said "Bob, Jason is here to pick you and David up and take you to live with him?"

It was like my stomach dropped. I didn't want to go, I felt safe here, protected, my world was about to get ugly again and I knew it. When we were done packing David and I went down stairs, my aunt hugged us with tears in her eyes and looked at Jason and told him, "Nothing better happen to these boys you get me? Do you understand?" He smiled and told her he would protect us with his life. I knew that was lie, all he wanted was the government money he could get off us.

So off we went, as we pulled out of the driveway my aunt and uncle waving at us and we both looking out of the back window with tears rolling down our cheeks and from out of nowhere we heard "Sit your assess down, turn around and shut up. I don't want to hear another word period!.

Well it appeared it was going to be a life of living hell all over again. And I could have never been more right. As we pulled back in to our house Jason looked into the back seat and said "Ok, here are the rules; I'm god and you do what I say and there won't be any problems".

We got in the door and David said "Why are we back here?" Jason looked at him and said "Mom will be here soon. She has asked me to bring you both back home. Marvin has left her and she wanted to make things right with you two. So, don't blow it this time. She told me how you two were acting and she said she just couldn't deal with it anymore." Confused "What did we do?" I said and He looked at me stating "You know what you done so shut up".

About that time mom pulled in and walked in the door and said "Hello boys, we need to talk so listen up; if anyone asks where I have been you must tell them that I have been here with both of you the whole time, and if you don't tell these people that, they will separate you two and you won't see one another ever again! So do what I say".

I wasn't about to let them separate me and David for no reason, so I said "OK" she smiled and said "That's my boy". I almost told her I'm not your boy remember, you told me you wish I was never born, but I couldn't say it instead I just smiled.

I got up and walked outside and at that moment I heard a puppy yipping, I ran down to road someone sat out the prettiest puppy I ever seen. I kept him and named him Yeller, because he was yelling so loud. He became my best friend in the world, the only one who would listen and be there for me. He followed me everywhere I went and waited for me outside the school gates every day.

We went swimming together and laid under the shady tree, he protected me from harm, one day mom grabbed me and Yeller snapped at her, because he knew she was hurting me. She kicked him and let me go, "Get rid of him or I will kill him" she said.

As days pasted my mom would disappear from time to time, but came back each time till one day she never came back.

Gary pulled up and said "Guys mom asked me and Andrea to stay with you for a while; she won't be able to come back for a long time". I said "No problem, we are use to it". As David sat on the sofa and I sat on the floor and Gary began telling us why she won't be back. "Guys, mom is in jail again, she was arrest for forgery and accessory to murder. She and Marvin robbed his uncle and Marvin shot him to death. They have mom on camera cashing checks they took from him".

I got up and walked outside and cheered so loud "She is gone, she is where she needs to be" but I felt so sorry that Marvin's uncle was dead but so was I. For so long I felt a sense of freedom but it didn't last long.

Gary said "Since mom turned evidence in on Marvin they are dropping the accessory to murder charge because she had no idea he was going to kill his uncle. She claimed she was in fear for her life from Marvin".

Mom will be released until her trial, my heart dropped I knew she was going to hell on earth. The next day mom came home and I was right, it didn't take her long before it came out, "Bob, you little bastard! Come here, why is my kitchen messed up?" David was with Gary at the doctor's office. And I knew I was going to be beaten so I ran across the street. The Swaney's were pulling out and I figured either Shelia or Peewee would be home, so I ran to their house.

"Is anyone home?" I yelled softly through the door, I knocked and no answer. The door was cracked at this point my mom stepped out on the porch screaming my name; "BOB COME HER RIGHT NOW!" scared I ran into their house. Hiding under the bed, about that time I heard them pull back in and I knew if they caught me in there, they wouldn't understand. I slid the window open and climb out, ran to woods behind their house. Sheila and Peewee's dad must have seen me; he yelled "Hey, you stop!" I ran deeper into woods and dropped under a fallen tree hoping he wouldn't see me.

I buried myself under the leaves hoping Mr. Swaney wouldn't walk around and see where I was hiding. I didn't want any trouble and if I got caught the police would have been called and once again the fear of me and David being separated terrified me. So I laid there still and quite as a mouse till he went away.

As he turned to walk away he said "Bobby, boy I know it was you. Stay away from my house and my kids" I dropped my head in shame, if only he knew why I was hiding, if only he knew what would of happened to me if my mom got her hands on me. I was doomed. To be looked at as a bad kid, something I will carry with me for the rest of my life.

One day Peewee came to the street where I was passing ball with David and he shoved me and asking "Why were you in my house? What did you take?" I looked at the ground and told him "I would never steal from you, I'm no thief and stop pushing me, ok. I am not like that and just leave me alone, you wouldn't understand if I told you".

Peewee with cocky smirk on his face "Try me" he said, so I looked at him and explained; my mom was drunk and angry and if she found me, she would have hurt me badly. She has been hurting me bad every day, I was hiding from her. I'm sorry, I was in your house but it was the safest place I could find. I didn't take anything, I swear".

At that moment Peewee drew back and punched me, I stumbled backwards, my nose bloody and I looked at him and said "I deserve that one, but no more" He drew back again and swung at me, I side stepped his fist and punched him in the eye, he dropped to the ground and started crying. His dad came running out "What is going on here?" I tried to explain but he wouldn't hear of it, so he took me to my mom and told her I attacked his son for no reason.

My mom looked at him "I'm so sorry, I will take care of it." I just knew I was going to get beat. When MR. Swaney left, my mom looked at me and said "Good job son, now you're acting like a Jenkins and I'm proud of you!" I was ashamed to call myself a

Jenkins, if that is what a Jenkins stood for I looked at my mom and said "Can I go now?" She said "Yes, go on back outside and play".

As I walked out the door Yeller was sitting on the porch waiting for me. "Come on Yeller let go to river" David yelled out if he could join us "Sure, come on" So we walked through the woods to the river. David went swimming as I sat on the river bank, "Yeller why am I here? What did I do to deserve living this way?" Yeller looked at me like he understood me and laid his head on my lap "It's ok boy" I said "One day, one day I will be bigger than the world, I will be save, I will be a major league baseball player or bigger.

The day was getting late "David, let's go home" and his response was "Just awhile longer Bob, please?" "David its dark and the snakes will be out swimming come on" he immediately stopped splashing around saying "Snakes! Did you say snakes?" he started crying "Bob, come get me?" I said "Just walk towards me, you will be fine." "No, no come get me please Bob?" So I took off my shoes "Ok David I'm coming."

So I went out and took him by the hand, "What was that!" he said "David it was a stick it's ok", as we got closer to the bank he ran out of the water left me standing there "I wasn't scared at all" he said and I responded "I know" with a grin on my face.

The walk home was long, it was dark and we could barely see through the woods "Bob wait for me" David said, "I'm right here David, I'm not going anywhere, I promise". As we approached the house there was car sitting in the driveway we have never seen before.

We walked in the door and there was one of Jason's friends sitting in my dad's chair, "Who are you?" I said as I walked by him, his reply was "My name is Kenny" as I walked into my room, I saw another one of Jason's friend. He was naked and so was my mom, they were having sex on my bed, "Get the hell out of here right now" I screamed, I ran to the closet in the hall and grabbed the shotgun and into the kitchen for a knife. I handed the knife to David. I said to David "Stand by the front door and if Kenny moves stab him".

I walked into the bedroom and put the shotgun in between the guy's eyes and told him "get the hell out!" Fear entered his face "Now Bob, put the gun down!" I looked at him cocked it back and said "I'm not going to let this happen in my dad's house, now get the hell out!" He stood up, at the foot of the bed saying "Let me have my clothes and I will leave?" I reached down and tossed his pants into the attic opening, "Leave without them", I said in a loud angry voice.

He walked in front of me the barrel pointing right at his head "Go on or I blow your damn head off", He ran outside. At about that time the police drove by "What are you doing out here with no clothes on son?" His buddy ran outside "These kids are crazy, he held a gun on him and his brother held a knife on me".

My mom went outside and told the cops "My boys did no such thing, these guys were trying to get in my house and my boys came home just in time to run them off", one of the officers asked "Then why is he naked" she said "Maybe he had other intentions for me!" The officer arrested him and said "You boys have a good night".

My mom turned and took me and David by the hand and walked us in the house when we entered the door my mom looked at me, climb up there and get me his pants. I went into the attic "Here mom" As I handed down his pants she went through his pockets and got his money, "Jack pot" she said and walked away.

The next day he came back "Hey, I want my pants back?" I had the shot gun in my hands as I tossed him his pants. "Where is my money?" I said "I don't know", my mom walked out on the porch "There wasn't any money." she said and I looked up at her with a confused look on my face, "Go inside Bob, I will handle this." I turned and went inside. As my mom walked inside she asked "Bob come here, you didn't tell him about the money did you?" "No mom, I didn't." I knew if I did she would beat me. "Ok, good boy" she said.

"David, you want to play outside with me?" He jumped up off the sofa "Sure what are we going to do?" "I was thinking about building a fort in woods, do you want to?" "Yeah, let's go".

When we approached the house we could hear my mom arguing with someone. As we turned the corner of the house, the police were there putting my mom in cuffs. "David come here? Don't let them see you" I pulled him back and we ran into the woods and hid from the police. Sitting beneath the tree, we waited for the coast to be clear.

When night fall came we started walking back to the house. The cops were gone and we climbed into the bedroom window and went into the kitchen, we haven't eaten all day. "So David," what would you like we have; chicken or hamburger, your choice" "Let's have chicken" He replied.

So here I went first time cooking chicken. I started remembering watching my grandmother cook in the kitchen and when I was done the colonel would have been proud.

After dinner we sat around in the living room watching "All in the Family" we laughed so hard, it was like nothing ever happened. It was routine for us, so we were use to it. As the night went on we got sleepy and decided it was bedtime. Finally my eyes were getting heavy and David has already fallen asleep on the sofa, I covered him up and went to bed myself.

The next morning David came running into my bedroom "Hey, wake up! Wake up! Someone is here!" I jumped out of bed and ran to the window, it was Gary. He and his wife Andrea were coming to live with us. He walked in and said "Bob, David; wake up! I'm home" as he started dropping their bags in the floor.

Finally, I thought to myself someone that can help me cook and clean little. Little did I know what was in store for me and David?

Gary said calmly "Come, sit down I have something to tell you" "What is it?" I asked, "Well guys, mom has been sentenced to five years in prison for forgery." And it felt like a fear was lifted off of me, "Finally!" I smiled and yelled out "Thank god!"

"What is this?" Andrea said "You're happy your mom went to prison?" "Yes, yes" I said repeatedly and ran outside full of life and happiness. When the morning went on I kept wondering what's for breakfast, and out of nowhere I hear "Hey Bob, what's for breakfast?" Stunned and surprised all I could say was "What would you like? How about some bacon and eggs" Gary replied "Sure, no problem".

So back to the kitchen I go. I asked Gary "Why don't she cook?" He said "She don't know how to cook!" I laughed, wow a female that couldn't cook that seemed kind of weird "Oh well" so off to cooking I went.

When everyone was done eating, I thought for sure that someone would volunteer to clean the kitchen and I was wrong again. So off to cleaning the kitchen I went, first putting left over biscuits on a plate and saving them for later, then ran some dish water and washed the dishes and wiped down the kitchen.

Swept and mopped the floor and finally I was done. It wasn't until I turned the corner and saw what the rest of the house looked like. I had spent an hour in the kitchen and now more time on the rest of the house; sweeping, dusting, and mopping. Wow, I was exhausted; they had tracked mud in from outside and had clothes scattered all over the house.

I picked up the clothes and put them in a pile on the sofa, I tried to fold them the best I could but they weren't my clothes. I didn't know how they wanted them.

Gary walked in and asked "Who sleeps in this room?", "I do Gary, why?" "Not anymore, I'm taking it" "Alright, no problem" I said as I went into the room and started packing my clothes and moving my stuff to the back bedroom.

When I got done moving my things, I went outside to look for David so we could have some fun. He was nowhere to be found; I looked everywhere, went to the neighbors, to the woods then I thought the river. I took off running towards the river, jumping over fallen trees and ducking under branches. As I approached the water there he was standing on the bank fishing. "Come Bob, join me?" With a deep breath "Ok David" so we both sat there in silence for a while.

As the night set in the fear grew stronger wondering what darkness lies ahead of me. David came into my room and said "Bob, I'm scared! Can I join you please?" He said over and over.

I looked at David and told him "sure come on"; with excitement in his face he climbed over me, under the covers and snuggled up close to me for the night.

The crickets outside my window kept me up all night, so I crawled out of bed and went out my window and climbed on the roof and laid there looking at the stars.

Making wish after wish wanting for god to take me away from this life, I was in, but no answer, no reply, no help! I thought to myself.

I whispered out "Ok god; no problem I will do it myself." as thoughts crossed my mind of just going to the bridge below the house and ending it all. I remembered who will protect David? So, I started planning making decisions, a twelve year old should not have to make decisions, I became a man that night and didn't even know it.

As the morning came through the trees I climb off the roof and went back to my room, laid down like nothing ever happened. At that moment my mother came into the room and said "Time to get up boys! It's time to get up!" She said it again: "If you don't get up right now I will whip your ass till you can't walk!"

"So David, what would you like to do now?" After sitting there for almost two hours "Bob, what's going to happen to us?" David said. With a sad look on his face, "What do you mean David?", "I have noticed that no one wants us! What's wrong with us Bob? Are we bad kids? Did we do something wrong?" Sitting there almost speechless, I didn't want David to feel that way, he deserves better than that.

I was determined to give it to him, "Well David, it's not us that are the problem, it's them. They just don't see how much of a great kid you are but I do, that's why I'm not going anywhere". A huge smile came on his face and said "We are brothers forever, aren't we?", "Yes, we are David, always no matter what you hear, no matter what", as we started walking back to the house the sun was setting in front of us and put my arm across David's shoulder and he tossed his across mine. "So what are we going to do with you?" I asked, "Well you could make me some cookies!" and he laughed.

I pulled his head down in a head lock; "You little punk" and he broke loose and started running with me hot on his trail, we ran up to the house and the door was open. There was no one home David stay here let me go check it out. "Ok Bob" I grabbed the axe from the wood pile and slowly went inside the house, went through every room and stepped into the kitchen, and yelled out "David, you can come in now" "Is everything ok?" David asked with fear in voice, "Yes just the same old stuff"

Gary took some food, the radio and the TV and left us with nothing, "David, do me favor find me some electrical wire ok?" "Sure Bob, no problem" so he took off looking for some wire as I went to the storage shed and pulled out an old radio and TV. I knew the radio worked but I was determined to get the TV working, so I took the old television we had for parts and started working on it.

I didn't know a thing about what I was doing, but I was going to fix it. After about two hours we had a TV one of the wires had broke off inside the power source and I found it the hard way, WOW what a way to find out shocked me so bad it made the hair on arms stand up.

"Here bob, here is your wire" David said with a smile on his face "Thanks little bro" I used the wire for an antenna. "David helps me carry the TV in the house. We sat it down on the TV table I built out of old lumber that was in the shed, plugged it up and "WOW" "Bob why does it look gray?" My reply was "It's a black and white TV David no color". "Oh ok" he replied.

About nine o'clock that night we heard a car pull in the driveway, it was a guy driving a huge car and he was dressed in black suit. He approached the door and knocked three times "Who is it?" I asked through the door, "My name is Robert and I'm looking for Debra. Is she home?" "She doesn't live here anymore, she lives in prison now", and in a soft voice I said "David go get me the gun?" "OK" he runs to the closet and brings me the gun.

I load it and aim it at the door "If he comes through that door I will shoot him", I told David "No one will ever hurt us again, I promise you". As I aim the gun towards the door the man said "Oh ok, sorry to bother you. Have a good evening" he said as he walked away and got into his car and drove off. I sat up all night making sure he didn't come back.

The next morning I got up "David lets go, buddy time to rise and shine come on", "Aaaawwww, Bob come on let me sleep just little while longer, please? "Nope, not a chance. Let's go buddy". Tired and sleepy I went into the kitchen "David what you want for breakfast?" he quickly replied "How about some pancakes", "Ok no problem" I stood in the kitchen and it hit me "Oh my god! David's birthday is coming up and I don't have anything for him". So my mind started turning I have heard David say he wanted a bike so that was my goal.

"He will have that bike if it's the last thing I do" I said to myself. : Breakfast is ready come and get it", he came running into the kitchen and immediately said "Where is the syrup at?" I looked around "I'm sorry David we don't have any but I have something better". I took some strawberry jam that we had on the table and ran hot water over the jar for about a minute until it was almost like syrup and put it on his pancakes and he loved it.

"Well David, it's off to school, you have missed enough school because of Gary now it's back to the books" it was going into April. School was about over and I started planning how I was going to get that bike for him. I started asking for work around the neighborhood and told each person it was to get my younger brother a bike.

One gentleman offered to give me an old bike he had. But my reply was "Sorry sir but I want him to have a new bike, it's his birthday present and I want it to be special but thanks anyway". "Well come back next week and I will have you some work to do" the older man said. "Ok and thank you sir." It was getting close to the end of the school day so I took off, me and Yeller and waited for David to get out, so we could walk home with him.

I could hear the bell ring, "Ok Yeller it's time for him to come out so watch for him ok." So we waited and waited and waited; about an hour later I said to Yeller to stay. I went into the school and David was sitting in the hall immediately I asked "David what's wrong?"

He looked up at me and said "I was waiting on you; I didn't see you outside so I got scared". "David I was by the big oak tree as always, I didn't see you. Well come on little brother let's get out of here", as we approached the gate Yeller ran and jumped up on David knocking him down, at this moment David started laughing so hard and saying "Ok, ok boy stop licking me". He jumped up and started running with Yeller hot on his trail.

We walked home very slowly and David wanted to stop and see one of his friends. When they finished talking about their day at school David looked at me with a smile, "Bob can we go fishing when we get home?" I asked "Do you have homework?" Immediately he replied "No, just some pictures to draw".

As we turned the corner and there was a car in the driveway, neither one of us knew who it was. Taking our time approaching the house I said "Wait here David" with concern in my voice, "Stay under the tree and wait for me to come and get you, ok!"

So I walked around, behind the house and looked into the kitchen window and to my surprise it was Jason, comfortably sitting at the table waiting for us.

I ran back to where David was sitting "David come on its Jason". "Great" David said with huge smile on his face and took off running rushed into the front door "Jason, Jason is that you?"

"Yes, I'm in the kitchen. Bob, David come in here and sit down" so we pulled out the chairs and sit down and Jason continued to tell us about how he was there to take us away. "Boys I'm sorry I haven't been here for you but I'm here now" David started crying and I didn't care either way, I knew he had a motive for taking us. I just didn't know what the motive was yet but I soon found out. And he continued "Guys go pack your things, you are going with me".

I didn't like it. I had a bad feeling about this but I was to the point were I just didn't care anymore so I decided to go. And he continued "Go ahead and pack". As we were packing Jason was going through the house finding things he could sell, at this point I dropped my head because I knew this wasn't going to be good.

"Ok boys, lets load up so we can get started" David climbed in the back seat and I climbed in the front seat, little did I know hell was waiting on the other side of town.

Made in the USA
Lexington, KY
20 June 2012